A Ticket to
China

Janet Riehecky

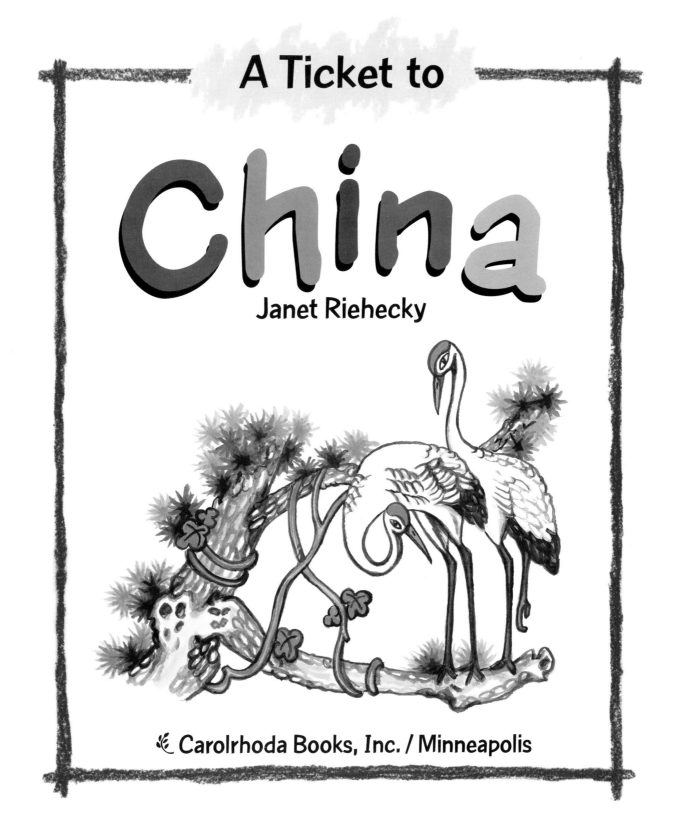

Carolrhoda Books, Inc. / Minneapolis

Photo Acknowledgments

Photos, maps, and artworks are used courtesy of: John Erste, pp. 1, 2–3, 18–19, 23, 25 (top), 29, 33, 39, 40–41, 41; Laura Westlund, pp. 4–5, 21; © Wolfgang Kaehler, pp. 6 (top), 8, 9, 11, 13, 14 (bottom), 16, 17 (both), 18 (left), 20, 22, 26, 30 (left), 37, 43 (top); © Eugene G. Schulz, pp. 6 (bottom), 15, 21, 24, 31, 40; Visuals Unlimited: (© Charles Preitner) p. 7, (© Jeff Greenberg) p. 14 (top), (© Steve McCutcheon) p. 18 (right), (© Jon Turk) p. 19, (© Will Trover) pp. 30 (right), 44, (© Robin Karpan) p. 34 (bottom), (© N. Pecnic) p. 39, (© Fritz Pölking) p. 45; ChinaStock: (© Dennis Cox) p. 10 (left), (© Liu Xiaoyang) p. 28, (© Christopher Liu) pp. 29, 32, 36, 38; © Brian A. Vikander, pp. 10 (right), 34 (top), 35 (bottom); Robert Fried Photography: (© Robert Fried) p. 12, (© Sophie Dauwe) pp. 27, 43 (bottom); Lejla Fazlic Omerovic, p. 25 (bottom); F. Botts/FAO, p. 35 (top); © Michele Burgess, p. 42; Cover photo © Wolfgang Kaehler.

Carolrhoda Books, Inc.
c/o The Lerner Publishing Group
241 First Avenue North
Minneapolis, Minnesota 55401 U.S.A.

Website address: www.lernerbooks.com

Library of Congress Cataloging-in-Publication Data

Riehecky, Janet.
    China / by Janet Riehecky.
      p.   cm. – (A Ticket to)
    Includes index.
    Summary: Discusses the people, geography, history, religion, language, customs, lifestyle, and culture of the third largest country in the world.
      ISBN 1-57505-140-0 (lib. bdg. : alk. paper)
      1. China—Juvenile literature. [1. China.] I. Title.
    II. Title: China.
    DS706.R545   1999
    951–DC21   98–21142

Manufactured in the United States of America
1 2 3 4 5 6 – JR – 04 03 02 01 00 99

Contents

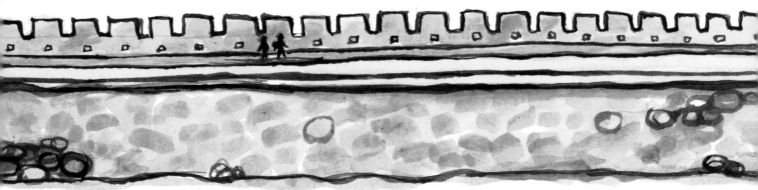

Welcome!

China is the world's third largest country. Only Russia and Canada are bigger. China lies on the biggest **continent** in the world—Asia. Beijing is China's **capital.**

China's east coast meets the Pacific Ocean. Thick forests and more of the Pacific Ocean lie to the south. High **mountains** and dry **deserts** separate China from countries to the north and west.

KAZAKHSTAN

KYRGYZSTAN

TAJIKISTAN

AFGHANISTAN

PAKISTAN

INDIA

NEPAL

TIAN SHAN

TAKLIMAKAN DESERT

KUNLUN SHAN

GANGDÎSE

HIMALAYAS

Mount Everest

BHUTAN

C

N

4

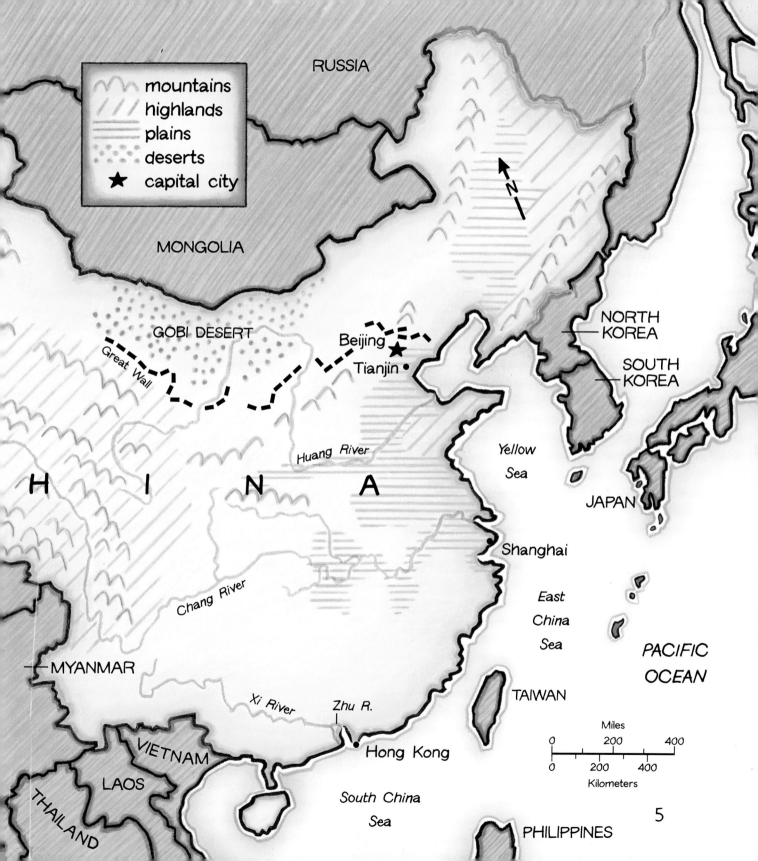

RUSSIA

MONGOLIA

mountains
highlands
plains
deserts
★ capital city

GOBI DESERT

Great Wall

Beijing
Tianjin •

N

NORTH
KOREA

SOUTH
KOREA

Huang River

C H I N A

Yellow
Sea

JAPAN

Shanghai

East
China
Sea

PACIFIC
OCEAN

Chang River

MYANMAR

TAIWAN

Xi River

Zhu R.

Hong Kong

VIETNAM

LAOS

THAILAND

South China
Sea

PHILIPPINES

Miles
0   200   400

0   200   400
Kilometers

5

Step Up!

China is like a giant staircase. The bottom step sits in the east. This part of China has farmland and rivers.

This small town lies near the Turpan Depression, China's lowest spot.

Wet fields called rice paddies cover farmland in eastern China.

The middle of China is the second step. This step has mountains, **basins**, and **plateaus**.

Map Whiz Quiz

Take a look at the **map** on pages four and five. Trace the outline of China onto a piece of paper. See if you can find the East China Sea. Mark this part of your map with an "E" for east. How about the country of Mongolia? Mark this with an "N" for north. Find the Huang River and the Chang River. Trace these rivers with the color blue. Next find the Great Wall of China. Color it red.

The Himalayas are the tallest mountains in the world.

Western China is the top step. High mountains and cold plateaus make this a tough place to live.

Two men steer their boat along a busy waterway.

Seas and Rivers

Some bodies of water that touch China's shores are called **seas.** The Yellow Sea is in the northeast. The South China Sea sits to the south. Can you guess where the East China Sea is?

Thousands of rivers run through China. The Chang River is the third-longest river in the world. The Huang River is sometimes called the Yellow River because of its color. Yellow dirt turns the river's water yellow!

People in China travel the water in boats. Folks catch and eat the tasty fish that swim the seas and rivers. Farmers use the rivers to water their crops.

Although China has plenty of water, some parts of the country are as dry as a bone! Scientists hope that planting trees will keep these dry deserts from spreading.

Chinese People

A girl holds her baby sister (top). *Ethnic Chinese kindergarteners enjoy a holiday* (left).

This woman belongs to one of China's many ethnic groups.

China has the biggest population of any country in the whole world. More than one billion people crowd into China's borders. Of every five people on our planet, one lives in China!

Almost all Chinese people are **ethnic Chinese**. They share **traditions,** a long history, and a rich culture. Can you guess what language they speak? Some Chinese people aren't ethnic Chinese. They have different languages and traditions.

Three Is a Family

A typical Chinese family enjoys a walk.

Most Chinese families are made up of two parents and one kid. There are so many people in China that the government made a rule that each family can only have one child. But that doesn't mean that a Chinese family is small.

Grandparents, aunts, uncles, and cousins make most Chinese families big. Relatives like to live near each other and to have meals together.

All in the Family

Here are the Chinese words for family members. Try them out on your family!

grandfather	*zufu*	(dzoo-foo)
grandmother	*zumu*	(dzoo-moo)
father	*fuqin*	(foo-chihn)
mother	*muqin*	(moo-chihn)
uncle	*shushu*	(shoo-shoo)
aunt	*ayi*	(ah-ee)
son	*er.zi*	(ER-dzeh)
daughter	*nuer*	(noo-er)
older brother	*ge.ge*	(GUH-guh)
younger brother	*de.de*	(DEE-dee)
older sister	*jie.jie*	(JEE-EH-jee-eh)
younger sister	*mei.mei*	(MAY-may)

In the City

In Shanghai, China's largest city, the streets get busy—and noisy (above)! Many families squeeze into these high-rise apartment buildings (right).

Hong Kong

Hong Kong is an island in the South China Sea. It was part of China until the 1800s, when Great Britain won it in a war. In 1997 Great Britain gave Hong Kong back to China. People celebrated this event with big parties.

Beep! Beep! Chinese cities are noisy, busy places. Millions of people live in Beijing, Shanghai, and Tianjin. The roads are jammed with people walking, biking, and driving!

Some city folks have houses, but most people live in small apartments. There are not enough apartments to go around. Two families sometimes share one little apartment.

On the Farm

Most Chinese live on farms in the country. In the warm southeast, farmers grow rice in wet fields called rice paddies. To the northeast, people raise wheat and soybeans.

A water buffalo helps a man plow his flooded rice paddy.

Farmers sell some of the food to the government. The rest goes to colorful markets.

Women plant rice seedlings (above). *Farmers can sell their extra food at street markets* (left).

Few Chinese own cars, so bicycles take people where they want to go (above left). *Boats carry people and goods along China's many waterways* (above).

Getting Around

Do you like to ride a bike? Folks who live in China's cities ride bicycles everywhere. There are so many bicycles that bike riders get stuck in traffic jams! In the country, animals help people travel. Some Chinese go down rivers and along coasts in boats. Trains carry people long distances.

Some Chinese live in portable houses called gers. They can travel without leaving home. They just bring their gers with them!

Long Ago in China

Emperors ruled China for 4,000 years. They were very rich, but most people were poor.

In 1911 the Chinese decided not to let emperors rule anymore. In 1949 the Communist Party took over. The Communist Party formed the People's Republic of China (PRC). The PRC tries to make sure that everyone has enough food to eat, a place to live, and clothes to wear.

More than 2,000 years ago, a Chinese emperor started work on the country's most famous feature—the Great Wall.

和国万岁　世界人民大团

A picture of a modern-day leader, Mao Zedong, decorates the Imperial Palace, which was built centuries ago.

But Chinese people have to do what the government says. Some Chinese people do not like this. They want to make up their own minds.

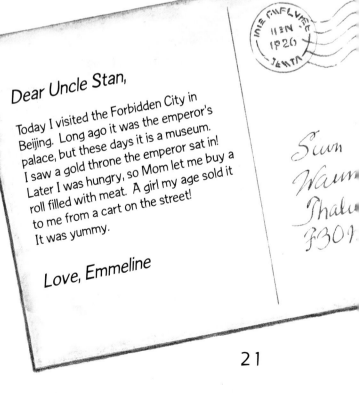

Dear Uncle Stan,

Today I visited the Forbidden City in Beijing. Long ago it was the emperor's palace, but these days it is a museum. I saw a gold throne the emperor sat in! Later I was hungry, so Mom let me buy a roll filled with meat. A girl my age sold it to me from a cart on the street! It was yummy.

Love, Emmeline

21

Speaking Chinese

In China, it is not what you say. It is also how you say it! Chinese words get their meanings from how a word is said. Here is an example. The word *ma* can mean mother or grasshopper.

Do you think these men are speaking Chinese?

No kidding! The meaning changes when a speaker's voice goes up or stays level.

People in different parts of China speak Chinese in different ways. In schools across China, kids learn to speak the same kind of Chinese. That way, people all over the country can use the same language to talk to one another.

If ma can mean mother or grasshopper, then what do you call a grasshopper's mother?

If you were a Chinese student, you would practice for many years to perfect your writing.

What a Character!

Chinese does not have an alphabet. Instead, a symbol called a **character** stands for each word. Drawing Chinese characters is a form of art in China. Writers use special brushes, black ink, and white paper.

Pinyin is another form of Chinese writing. Pinyin Chinese words are written with letters like English is.

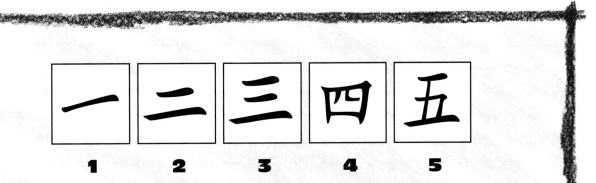

Write the numbers 1 through 5 in Chinese characters.

You will need: a paintbrush, black paint, and a sheet of paper to paint on. Use the very tip of the paintbrush for the thin lines, and press a little harder to make the fat lines. You may want to practice making the fat, thin, and medium lines. It is harder than it looks!

Young Chinese people respect older people's ideas. When this baby gets older, she will ask her grandmother for advice.

Faith and Respect

Older people are respected in China. The Chinese believe that because older people have lived for a long time, they know a lot about life. Younger people ask their grandparents for advice when times are confusing.

Often the older person has a helpful answer. Chinese people also believe in sharing, cooperation, and hard work.

The Biggest Buddha

Some people in China believe in the teachings of the Buddha, a religious leader who lived a long time ago. The world's biggest statue of the Buddha is carved in the side of a cliff in southern China. The statue sits at a place where three rivers meet. It took workers about 100 years to carve! It is so big that two people can stand up next to one another in each ear. Two people can sit side by side on one of the statue's toenails!

Happy New Year!

Chinese New Year is a special holiday. Everybody wants the new year to have a happy start. A huge celebration lasts for three days. Parades fill the streets, and people make huge puppets dance. A lion puppet at the beginning of the parade scares

A group of drummers forms a dragon in a parade on Chinese New Year.

People walk on stilts for a crowd of partygoers.

away bad spirits. A long paper dragon puppet ends the parade.

Water Dragon

Why does a dragon puppet end the parade? In Chinese stories, dragons are not scary monsters. They are wise and helpful. Dragons in Chinese legends bring water, which Chinese people need to grow crops. So in China, a dragon puppet is a lucky way to end a parade.

Chinese elementary-school students do exercises before the day's lessons begin. These kids are rolling their eyes to the tune of a song!

School Days

There's time for play during the school day at this kindergarten.

Reading, writing, and arithmetic. Does that sound familiar? That is what Chinese students learn in school! They also spend part of the day cleaning the school. Lots of schools have gardens where kids grow vegetables. The students learn to pitch in and help out.

Most Chinese children start school at age 6 and end school at age 12. After that, they might help their parents on a farm. But some kids keep going to school. Teenagers might go to college, but most take jobs.

These girls are dressed for an after-school musical performance.

Story Time

The Chinese have many wonderful stories. Some tell of exciting adventures. Others are long poems or **folktales**. Some stories are new, but many are very, very old. Chinese people like folktales that teach lessons of sharing or of good behavior.

An ancient illustration from a famous Chinese story, the Romance of the Three Kingdoms.

The Magic Goldfish

Once upon a time, there lived a young woman named Ye Shen. Ye Shen had a mean stepmother. Ye Shen had to do all the housework. The wicked stepmother even killed Ye Shen's pet goldfish! Ye Shen was so sad that she kept the fish's bones to remind her of her pet.

One day Ye Shen learned that the bones could grant wishes! When everyone in town went to a festival, Ye Shen had to stay home. She had no nice clothes to wear. The magic fish bones saved the day. The bones gave her such beautiful clothes and shoes that the king fell in love with her. She left the party before the king could learn her name, but he was left with one tiny slipper. . . .

Can you guess how this story ends?

Hint: Think of the story *Cinderella!*

33

Clothes

People in China put on all different kinds of clothes. Lots of people choose comfortable shirts or

In ancient China, rich people wore beautiful silk robes (above), *but poor people dressed in loose cotton clothes* (left).

pants that are easy to work in. Some city folks wear suits and ties or dresses. Others love the latest fashions.

Silkworms spin the fine threads that Chinese craftspeople weave into silk.

Silk

The Chinese invented silk, a smooth, shiny fabric. Skilled workers unwind the cocoons of silkworms, a kind of caterpillar. People weave silk from the thin strands of the cocoons.

Many Chinese kids wear the same types of clothing that you wear. Some like to put on uniforms, too.

These students from Beijing can play table tennis in their school playground.

Playtime

In the morning, some Chinese gather in parks or in empty streets to practice **martial arts**. The graceful motions are good exercise. They are also useful for self-defense. Chinese kids love to fly kites, too.

Table tennis and gymnastics are very popular in China. Special schools help young people practice their sport. Some of these students become professional or Olympic athletes.

Many Chinese people like to come to the park for morning exercises.

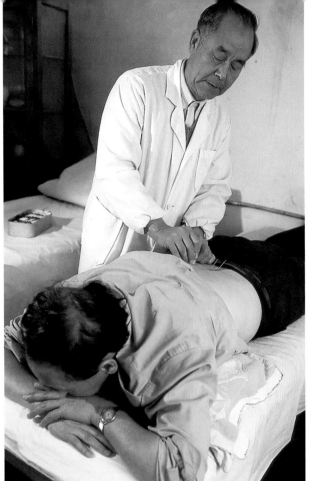

A doctor uses acupuncture needles to help heal a patient. Do you think he is feeling better yet?

Doctors

Would you think that sticking a thin needle into your skin could cure a headache? A Chinese doctor would think so! This practice is called acupuncture. The Chinese believe that more than 100 diseases can be cured with acupuncture. But do not try this at home!

Only experts know how to do acupuncture right. Some Chinese doctors also give out pills and use high-tech machines to help sick people get better.

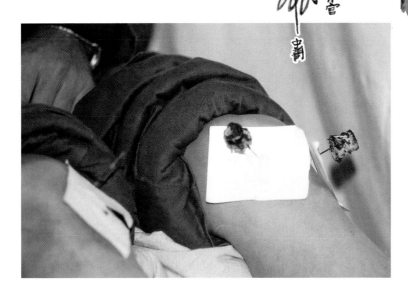

Charts show doctors where to put the needles—whether in people's arms (above) *or legs* (left).

An open-air marketplace sells Chinese fruits and vegetables.

Shopping for Food

Most people in China do not own refrigerators. So the Chinese go shopping at outdoor markets every day for fresh food. They might spend a lot of time looking for the cheapest price. Some of the food might be pickled, dried, or salted to keep it from going bad.

Not all Chinese eat the same types of food. In the south, farmers grow a lot of rice. People who live nearby eat rice at just about every meal. In the north, where wheat is a major crop, folks make the grain into noodles. Fresh cooked vegetables are important parts of meals across China.

Meal Time!

A tasty noodle dish waits for diners to dig in.

A popular way to prepare a meal in China is to stir-fry it. First a cook chops meat and vegetables into bite-size bits. The next step is frying the raw food over a very hot fire. The cook stirs the food around in a big pan so that it does not burn while it fries. The big pan is called a wok.

Eating With Chopsticks

Almost no one in China uses knives or forks. They use chopsticks! Chopsticks are long, thin sticks held in one hand. Experts use them like a pair of fingers. It takes a long time to learn how to use chopsticks well!

A chef (above) makes dumplings, a popular Chinese food. For Chinese kids (right), chopsticks are easy to use. Can you eat with chopsticks?

New Words to Learn

basin: A deep depression in the land, often with a lake at the bottom. Basins are found near mountain ranges.

capital: A city where the government is located.

character: Instead of letters, some languages, such as Chinese and Japanese, use a picture or symbol that stands for a whole word or for a word sound.

continent: Any one of seven large areas of land. The continents are Africa, Antarctica, Asia, Australia, Europe, North America, and South America.

desert: A dry, sandy region.

ethnic Chinese: A person related to an early Chinese people called the Han.

More than 8,000 life-size, clay warriors guard the tomb of one Chinese emperor.

folktale: A timeless story told by word of mouth from grandparent to parent to child. Many folktales have been written down in books.

map: A drawing or chart of all or part of the earth or sky.

martial arts: Ways of fighting and of protecting oneself. Martial arts—which were started in China, Japan, and Korea—include judo, kendo, aikido, and karate.

mountain: A part of the earth's surface that rises high into the sky

plateau: A large area of high, level land.

sea: A body of water that is partly enclosed by land.

tradition: A way of doing things—such as preparing a meal, celebrating a holiday, or making a living—that a group of people practice.

The Chinese people are proud of the giant pandas that live in the bamboo forests of southern China.

New Words to Say

Beijing	BAY-JING
Buddha	BOO-dah
Chang River	CHANG RIH-vehr
ger	GUHR
Himalaya	HIH-mah-LAY-uh
Huang River	HWANG RIH-vehr
pinyin	PIN-YIN
Shanghai	SHANG-HI
Tianjin	TEEAHN-JIHN
Turpan Depression	toor-PAHN dih-PREH-shen
Ye Shen	YEH SHEN

More Books to Read

Fyson, Nance Lui and Richard Greenhill. *A Family in China.* Minneapolis: Lerner Publications, 1985.

Haskins, Jim. *Count Your Way Through China.* Minneapolis: Carolrhoda, 1987.

Hong, Lily Toy. *The Empress and the Silkworm.* Morton Grove, Illinois: Albert Whitman, 1995.

Louie, Ai-Ling. *Yeh-Shen: A Cinderella Story from China* (retold). New York: Philomel Books, 1982.

McKenna, Nancy Durrell. *A Family in Hong Kong.* Minneapolis: Lerner Publications Company, 1987.

Pitkanen, Matti. *The Children of China.* Minneapolis: Carolrhoda, 1990.

New Words to Find